Rya

This edition published by
Coles, Canada
by arrangement with Twin Books

© 1993 Twin Books Ltd

Produced by
TWIN BOOKS
Kimbolton House
117A Fulham Road
London SW3 6RL
England

Directed by CND – Muriel Nathan-Deiller
Illustrated by Van Gool-Lefèvre-Loiseaux

ISBN: 1 85469 925 3

Printed in Hong Kong

"'VAN GOOL'S'"

Goldilocks

TWIN BOOKS

Once there was a little
girl whose hair was so
golden and curly, she
was called Goldilocks.
She was very lively
and curious, which
often got her into
trouble at home. One
morning her mother
discovered her reaching
up into the kitchen
cupboard for some jam.

"Goldilocks," she
scolded, "get off that
chair! You could fall and
hurt yourself. Why don't
you go and play outside?"

In a house not far away, Baby Bear was sitting down to his breakfast. But he was in tears! When he tried to eat his porridge, it was far too hot. "Never mind," said his parents kindly, "we'll go for a walk until your porridge cools down. And, perhaps we'll find some berries."

So the three bears put on their scarves and set off for the woods.

"Wait," cried Baby Bear, "I have left the basket behind!" And he ran back to the house to fetch it.

"Don't forget to close the door," called Papa Bear. But . . . Baby Bear forgot!

A short while later, Goldilocks, who had wandered away from home, saw the bear family's cottage.

"Oh!" she cried, "What a pretty house. I wonder who lives here? I must go and have a closer look."

Goldilocks knocked loudly on the door but there was no answer. Then she saw it was ajar, so she peeped inside. Behind the door were three brooms: a large broom, a medium-sized one and a little one. And on the table there was a steaming bowl of porridge. It smelled so good that Goldilocks immediately felt hungry.

Forgetting her manners, she pushed open the door and went in. On the table she saw not only one, but three bowls of porridge: a large one, a medium-sized one and a small one. In the middle of the table there was also a big pot of porridge. She sat down and tried some porridge from the large bowl, but it was much too hot!

"I can't eat this!" said Goldilocks. So she tried the next bowl. It was much too cold. Finally, she ate from the smallest bowl. "This is just right!" she exclaimed, and greedily finished it all. Then she began to look around the cottage with interest.

"This house has three of everything," thought Goldilocks, as she looked at the candles on the sideboard. By the fireplace she saw two armchairs and a small rocking chair. She went to look more closely.

Of course, she knew better, but she climbed onto the largest chair and jumped up and down. It was hard and springy. When she had made a big dent in the cushion, she moved to the medium-sized armchair. It was soft and lumpy.

Then, Goldilocks sat in the little
rocking chair and rocked as hard as
she could. What fun!
But, she was going so fast . . .

. . . the rocking chair tipped over backwards. She tumbled onto the floor, and the little chair broke into pieces. "Oh dear!" cried Goldilocks as she picked herself up. "Someone is going to be very cross with me."

Goldilocks thought it was time to go home, but then she noticed a staircase. "I must investigate," she decided as she climbed the stairs. "It will only take a minute."

At the top of the stairs she pushed open the door and saw a comfortable bedroom. In it were three beds of different sizes: large, medium and small. "Just like the bowls and chairs," she thought, as she entered the room.

The beds looked so inviting that Goldilocks wanted to curl up and go to sleep. She climbed onto the largest bed, but it felt much too hard. Then she tried the middle-sized bed, but it was too soft and lumpy.

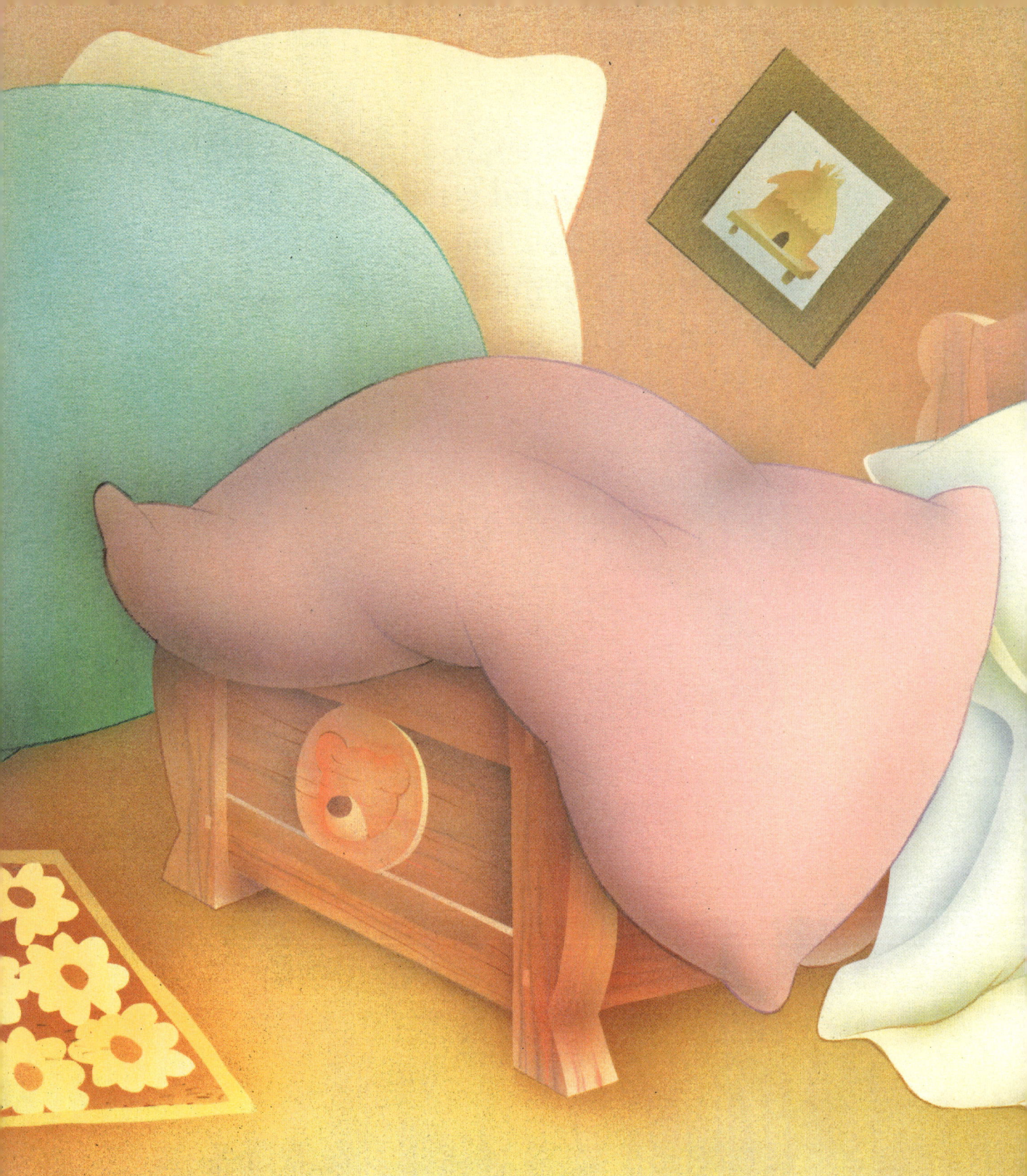

Finally, she lay down on the little bed. It felt
just right! In a moment she was fast asleep.

Meanwhile, the three bears were having a pleasant walk in the woods. Mama Bear was gathering flowers and Baby Bear was picking blackberries. Papa Bear was looking for honey, but the bees became angry and flew out to scare him away. "Let's go home!" cried Papa Bear.

"My porridge must be cool by now," said Baby Bear on the way home. "I can't wait to eat it! I'm hungry." His parents, too, were ready for breakfast, so they all hurried back.

When they reached their house, the three bears stopped in surprise. The door was wide open! Papa Bear frowned at Baby Bear. "Didn't I tell you to close the door?" he said.

"I thought I had," answered Baby Bear.

"Perhaps it didn't catch," suggested Mama Bear, "and the wind blew it open."

But once the three bears were inside, they knew immediately that someone had been there. What a mess!

"Someone's been eating my porridge!" growled Papa Bear.

"And someone's been eating my porridge, too!" added Mama Bear crossly.

"Someone has been eating my porridge and has finished it all up!" cried Baby Bear.

When they looked into the living room, Mama Bear
exclaimed, "Someone has been climbing on my chair!"
Papa Bear said, "And jumping on mine!"
Baby Bear started crying loudly. "Someone has sat on
my chair and broken it into pieces!" he wailed.

Mama Bear spooned out a new bowl of
porridge for Baby Bear, while Papa Bear
continued to look around. "I mean to
find out what happened here," he said
angrily.

"I'm tired," yawned Baby Bear, when
he had finished his porridge.

Mama Bear took Baby Bear upstairs. But when she opened the bedroom door, she called out to Papa Bear, "Come, quickly." Papa Bear ran up as fast as his heavy legs could carry him. "Look at this shambles!" cried Mama Bear, as Baby Bear peeked around her skirt.

Hesitantly, all three bears walked into the bedroom. The covers on the two larger beds were rumpled, not neatly in place as they had been that morning.

Baby Bear went over to his bed, as both his parents exclaimed, "Someone has been sleeping in our beds!"

"Someone's been sleeping in my bed, too!" cried Baby Bear excitedly. "And she's still there!"

Mama and Papa Bear rushed over to see the intruder.
At that very moment Goldilocks woke up. Once they saw
that it was a pretty little girl who had made a mess in
their house, the bears' anger vanished. Baby Bear was
quite delighted. But Goldilocks, as you can imagine,
was very frightened to see three bears looking at her!

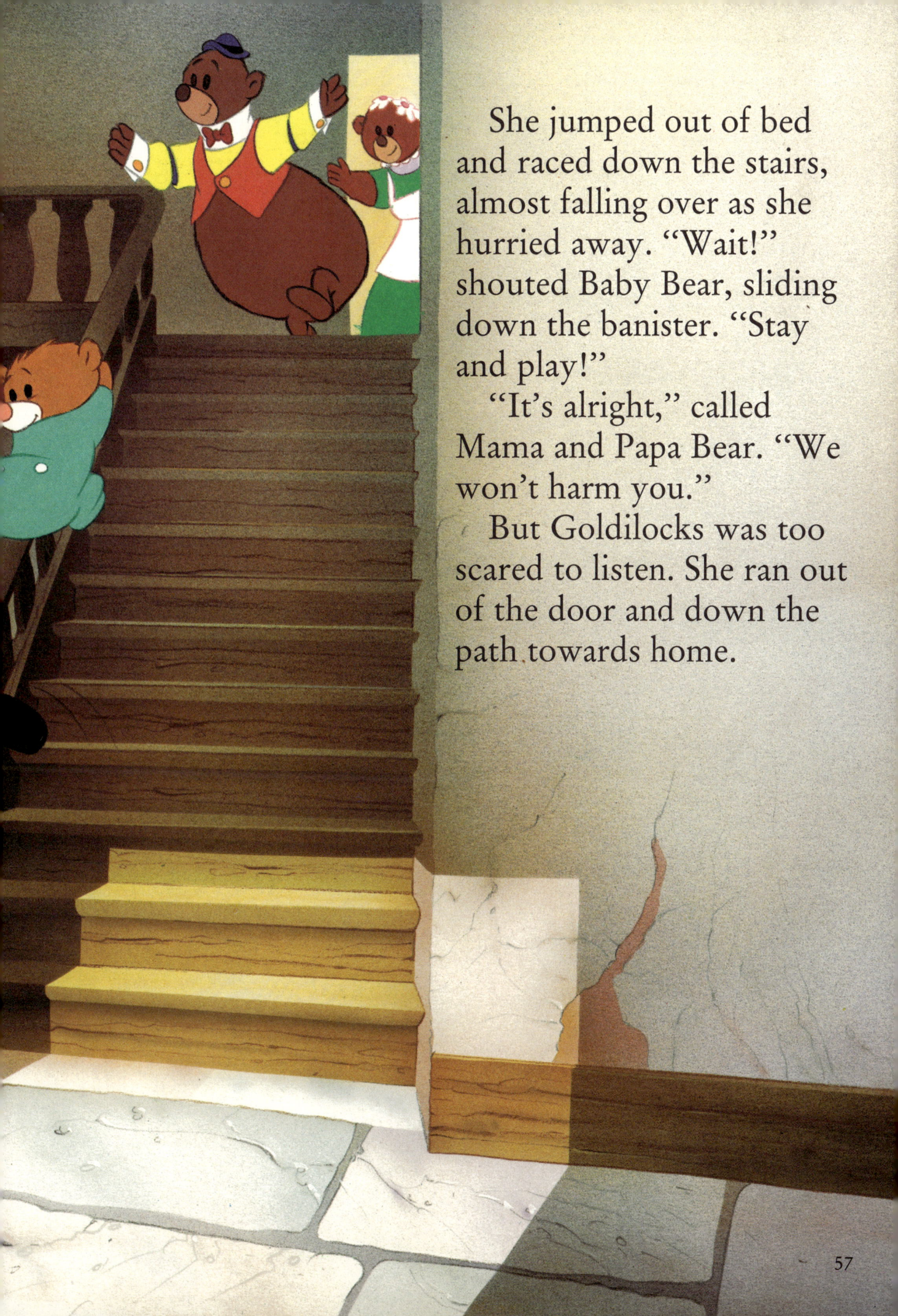

She jumped out of bed and raced down the stairs, almost falling over as she hurried away. "Wait!" shouted Baby Bear, sliding down the banister. "Stay and play!"

"It's alright," called Mama and Papa Bear. "We won't harm you."

But Goldilocks was too scared to listen. She ran out of the door and down the path towards home.

Mama and Papa Bear started to laugh when they thought how frightened they'd been by a little girl. But they stopped when they saw Baby Bear's expression.

"Don't be sad. One day soon, we'll invite her back to play."

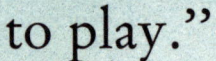

Goldilocks was nearly home. She was out of breath but relieved to be safe. "How angry Mother would be if she knew," she thought. "Next time I decide to pay a visit, I'll wait to be invited in." And so she did.